M...

Most b...
complex ...~~of theoretical~~ rather than practical. But *The Truth About Evocation of Spirits* clearly explains the process so that you can truly understand how to set up a "cosmic video-phone" to communicate with gods, goddesses, spirits (including kings, elementals, princes, principalities, and genii), and ghosts of the dead.

The Truth About Evocation of Spirits addresses and clears up the common misconceptions about evocation. It also tells you everything you need to know in order to successfully evoke nonphysical entities: the tools you'll need, pitfalls to avoid, how to choose the entity you wish to evoke, and step-by-step instructions for performing an evocation.

Let *The Truth About Evocation of Spirits* show you how beings of the astral plane can help you achieve your goals and make positive changes in your life!

About the Author

Donald Michael Kraig is the author of *Modern Magick*, one of the most popular books on magick ever published, and is the former Editor-in-Chief of the *Llewellyn New Times* and FATE magazine. An Aries with a grand trine in fire, he graduated from UCLA with a degree in philosophy. He has worked as a musician and a sleight-of-hand magician and has taught numerous classes on Western and Eastern metaphysical topics. He regularly writes articles for several magazines.

To Write to the Author

If you wish to contact the author or would like more information about this book, please write to the author in care of Llewellyn Worldwide and we will forward your request. Both the author and publisher appreciate hearing from you and learning of your enjoyment of this book and how it has helped you. Llewellyn Worldwide cannot guarantee that every letter written to the author can be answered, but all will be forwarded. Please write to:

Donald Michael Kraig
c/o Llewellyn Worldwide
P.O. Box 64383-393, St. Paul, MN 55164-0383, U.S.A.

Please enclose a self-addressed, stamped envelope for reply,
or $1.00 to cover costs.
If outside U.S.A., enclose international postal reply coupon.

Free Catalog from Llewellyn

For more than 90 years Llewellyn has brought its readers knowledge in the fields of metaphysics and human potential. Learn about the newest books in spiritual guidance, natural healing, astrology, occult philosophy and more. Enjoy book reviews, new age articles, a calendar of events, plus current advertised products and services. To get your free copy of *Llewellyn's New Worlds of Mind and Spirit*, send your name and address to:

Llewellyn's New Worlds of Mind and Spirit
P.O. Box 64383-393, St. Paul, MN 55164-0383, U.S.A.

LLEWELLYN'S VANGUARD SERIES

The Truth About

EVOCATION
OF SPIRITS

by Donald Michael Kraig

Author of
Modern Magick

1994
Llewellyn Publications
P.O. Box 64383, St. Paul, MN 55164-0383
U.S.A.

For permissions, or for serialization, condensation, or for adaptations, write the Publisher.

First Edition
First Printing, 1994

International Standard Book Number:
1–56718–393–X

LLEWELLYN PUBLICATIONS
A Division of Llewellyn Worldwide, Ltd.
P.O. Box 64383, St. Paul, MN 55164-0383

Other Books by Donald Michael Kraig

Modern Magick

The Magical Diary

Llewellyn Publications is the oldest publisher of New Age Sciences in the Western Hemisphere. This book is one of a series of introductory explorations of each of the many fascinating dimensions of New Age Science—each important to a new understanding of Body and Soul, Mind and Spirit, of Nature and humanity's place in the world, and the vast unexplored regions of Microcosm and Macrocosm.

Please write for a full list of publications.

WHY MAGIC?

Some of you who have picked up this book are already practitioners of magic in one or more of its many varieties. Others are intrigued by the idea of magic and the possibility of evoking spirits. But a more important question needs to be asked first: *Why should we practice magic?*

There are many answers to this question. Obviously magic—the ability to make positive changes in our environment according to our will by means not yet understood by traditional Western science—can help to improve our lives. But reading, higher education, getting a new job, having better eating habits and getting enough exercise can also improve our lives. So the question remains: *Why magic?*

The answer is that performing magical rituals does more than simply change our external world, it also changes our internal make-up. The regular practice of magic can actually alter our body's chemistry.

Does this sound far-fetched? It's not. Consider the effect that just thinking about food can have on your body. Your mouth starts to salivate. The brain sends out chemicals that directly or indirectly stimulate appetite and start acid flowing to the stomach. Blood also flows toward the stomach. Or consider the effect that thinking about sex has on the body! The glands begin to produce chemicals that prepare the body for sex. The brain, stimulated by sexual thoughts, also produces chemicals known as *endorphins*. Endorphins are so powerful that they rival heroin as a pain blocker.

Practicing magic also produces changes in our body chemistry. We become smarter, more astute and more clever as a result of using our mind in new and different ways. We also attune ourselves to the psychic world and become more open to the nonphysical world sometimes called the astral plane. Regular performance of magical rituals keeps the chemicals that create these changes constantly flowing through our bodies. We change and evolve.

Science shows that humans are the result of millions of years of evolution. It is naive to assume that evolution has stopped. In fact, we are in the process of becoming *more than human*, of being better than we currently are.

Therefore, by performing magic we are helping the human race to improve. Some might say that it is our *obligation* to help the human race improve. In that case, the performance of magic by those who know its techniques should be considered as something more than simply a way to get ahead. Magic becomes a sacred obligation, one that is as powerful and as important as honesty, justice and charity.

Magic has been practiced since the beginning of unrecorded time. The earliest legends and stories are filled with magic. The world's religions are filled with magic. Magic is more than just an obligation—it is our birthright! With books such as this one, *Modern Magick* and many of the books published by Llewellyn Publications, the techniques of magic become available to everyone. See the end of this book for information about other books from Llewellyn.

EVOCATION IS PART OF OUR NATURE

Besides having an interest in magic, people since the beginning of time have asked, "Is this all there is? Is there nothing more to human existence than struggle, survival and procreation?" In virtually every culture that has ever existed on this planet, the answer to that question has been a resounding "No!"

According to anthropologists and archaeologists, the earliest people honored or even worshiped the spirits of those in their families and clans who were deceased. It would naturally follow that those who were important in the family or clan would require special treatment and reverence. This can be seen in the mummification practices of the ancient Egyptians and Mayans.

As those early humans looked at the sky at night they began to wonder who created those faraway lights. In fact, they must have wondered who created the nearby lights of the Sun and Moon. They also must have wondered who created the Earth and themselves.

Thus began a search that started in our dim past and continues until today. Early people believed in beings who were not part of our physical existence. At first this included gods, goddesses and the spirits of the dead. This expanded to include numerous gods and goddesses who controlled every aspect of life. Some of these gods became of lesser importance than the main gods and goddesses, and the mighty pantheons of deities of so many ancient cultures developed.

Cultures both small and large rose and fell. The deities of a fallen culture became the devils of those that followed it. Since these devils could not be as powerful as the new gods, they were downgraded even further, as were some of the minor gods (and sometimes even the major ones) of the newer culture. Thus was born the three basic divisions of nonphysical entities: gods and goddesses, spirits (including kings, elementals, princes, principalities, genii, etc.) and the ghosts, or surviving personalities, of the dead.

ARE THEY REAL?

If gods and goddesses, spirits and ghosts developed as a result of our interpretation of the universe, how can they be real? Are they not mere figments of our imagination?

There are two answers to this. First, merely because we were not *aware* that they were there does not make them an invention of our minds. Few if any people in Europe were aware that the American continents existed before the 16th century. That did not make North and South America imaginary, simply unknown.

Further, merely because our understanding of nonphysical entities has changed does not mean that we have created a false reality. All it means is that the more we learn about them the more we can correctly identify them. To extend the above analogy, look at some of the earliest maps drawn by those who visited the Americas. They drew the maps as best they could, but the charts were filled with errors. Today's maps are far more accurate, just as our understanding of nonphysical entities is far more accurate.

Second, some theorists believe that since it took humanity a while to appreciate the existence of these entities, they must be mental creations. In this case, such nonphysical entities are said to be *archetypes*. Do not, however, confuse such an archetype with a simple, idealized model (as in the expression, "He was an archetypal teacher."). The meaning of the word, based on the theories of the great psychologist C. G. Jung, is quite different. He proposed that there is a level to our minds, which he called the *collective unconscious*, through which all humans are linked. Our collected minds may then create something we need (such as a god or goddess, spirit or ghost), but that creation would then have its own existence apart from what any individual thought. In short, although we, as humans united through our collective unconscious, may have in some way created nonphysical entities, they now have an independent existence of their own.

In either case they function as independent entities, and that is all that matters to us here.

(Of course, the philosophy known as *materialism* denies anything that is nonphysical, but chances are you would not be reading this if you believed in that limiting philosophy.)

EVOCATION AND INVOCATION

Many people use the words *evocation* and *invocation* interchangeably. To those who actually practice these techniques, however, they are quite different.

Invocation is the process of inviting an entity to take over and use your body to communicate with the physical world. This has been popularized over the centuries by a variety of names, the most recent being *mediumship* and *channeling*. Due to the fact that invocation is so easy to fake, the procedure of invocation has been mocked and insulted. In its most common forms, this is justified. Its history—especially over the last 150 years—is rife with dishonesty. Although there is not enough space to discuss the matter here, there are methods of invocation that are positive, sound and not open to flim-flammery. People who do these kinds of magical invocations do not do so to make money or obtain numerous followers, including Hollywood personalities, who merely wish to satisfy their desire to be part of the latest spiritual fad. Rather, they perform invocations to help acquire positive qualities and characteristics or obtain spiritual information that is not available elsewhere.

As a general rule, gods and goddesses are *in*voked while other nonphysical entities are *e*voked. Thus, if someone wanted additional strength, he or she might invoke Thor or Mars. If that person wanted more wisdom he or she might invoke Thoth or Hermes.

You may be able to see some immediate problems with invocation, not even counting the regrettable fakery that goes on by some of the more public performers. For example, a person can become "ego-inflated" and overly self-righteous from "being one with a god." Another problem is that the invoker may not check to see that he or she is actually invoking the entity desired and become confused with information that was not desired. You can probably see some other difficulties.

Evocations, on the other hand, are far safer. You do not bring a nonphysical entity into you. Rather, you simply move to a space where you and that entity can communicate. In effect, you set up a cosmic telephone booth and use a videophone so you can see and communicate with the entity you evoke.

A POOF AND A CLOUD OF SMOKE

We've all seen it in a movie or comic book. Maybe we read about it in some potboiler novel. A small boy awkwardly reads some weird words and "poof!" out comes some entity to do the boy's bidding. Or a berobed wizard waves his wand and a spirit rises from a cloud of smoke to obey the wizard's commands.

It sure looks nice in the movies, but it doesn't happen that way.

At this point, many practicing magicians reading this may react negatively. "Who does he think he is, telling us that evocation is not the way I always thought it would be? I want to see a spirit appear in a cloud of incense."

When I was beginning my studies of magic I, too, used to think that when I was ready I would go for the "poof and cloud of smoke." But others whom I respect showed me the error of my assumptions. For example, the late Dion Fortune (nee Violet Firth), former member of the Hermetic Order of the Golden Dawn, founder of the Society of the Inner Light and one of the great contemporary occultists, wrote in her book, *Aspects of Occultism:*

> In the great majority of cases of evocative magick, the form is built up on the astral and can only actually be seen by the clair-

voyant, though any sensitive person can feel its influence.

The initiated magician is usually, unless engaged in some special experiment or research, content to evoke to visible appearance on the astral, depending upon his psychic powers for communication with the entity evoked. He does not go to the trouble to evoke to visible appearance on the physical because, if he is an adequate psychic, astral appearance serves his purpose just as well; in fact, better, because it is more congenial to the nature of the beings . . . and places less limitation upon their activities.

CLEARING THE MISCONCEPTIONS

So now that we know that when we do an evocation we do not drag some entity, screaming and complaining, onto the physical plane, let's look at some more of the common misconceptions about evocation and clear them up.

1. *Some of the ancient books known as* grimoires *claim that by following their instructions you can evoke an entity onto the physical plane. If you don't really do that, why would they say that you do?*

This is a fairly easy question to answer. The *grimoires* (pronounced "grim-wahrz") were books of instruction on magic. Most are medieval although their sources are much older. When you read these books (such as the *Goetia*—part of a larger book called *The Lesser Key of Solomon*—and *The Greater Key of Solomon*) you will find that they do not say that you will evoke the entity onto the physical plane, the level of reality where we live and breathe. Rather, they say that by following the instructions in those books you can evoke an entity to physical appearance. That is, if you perform the rituals as indicated you will be able to view and communicate with them. This happens when you see the entity on what is called the *astral plane*.

2. *Why are there usually at least two people present when doing an evocation?*

Nobody can do everything, or it may be more appropriate to say that nobody can do everything equally well. Perhaps you have natural talents as a magician, the person who performs the ritual and asks questions of the entity evoked. Perhaps you have more natural talents to be a *seer* (what Dion Fortune called a *clairvoyant* in the above quotation), the person who looks onto the astral plane, the area where you can see an entity during an evocation. Usually, one person will function as the magician while the other person functions strictly as the seer. Sometimes one person may do both, but splitting the labor is easier and often more efficient.

3. Why, in the Goetia, *is a circle drawn within a triangle as the place where an entity is supposed to manifest?*

The word *grimoire* is similar in meaning to our "grammar" when we are discussing a textbook. When you look at an original copy of a grimoire—not the sterilized and perfectly typeset copies you usually find at bookstores and in libraries—you will see poor handwriting and simplistic drawings. They are obviously nothing more than somebody's notes. For example, when you compare the perfect images drawn in modern versions of the *Goetia* to the original drawings, you will see that the artist of the original had no sense of dimension. What is shown as horizontal could also have been something hung in a vertical manner.

So what was that magician (or his scribe) indicating in that book? The circle within the triangle signifies a magic mirror (more on this later). Such a mirror is a physical doorway to the astral plane. Two excellent occultists, Nelson and Anne White, agree with this in their book, *Secret Magick Revealed*.

4. The grimoires show certain designs called pentacles *or* seals *that are used in evocation. How do they work?*

For this form of magic (some say for all forms of magic) it is imperative that the seer achieve an altered state of consciousness. It is this altered state that allows the seer to look into the astral plane through the mirror and see what is there. In an evocation, however, we want the seer to establish contact with just one entity.

Now pause a second and look around the room you are in. There may be hundreds of things lying about. Even if you are in an altered state of mind, just looking into the room may not draw your attention to the one object in that room that is important for you at this time. Police detectives specialize in trying to find one or more things at the scene of a crime that can help solve the case. That one important clue may be hidden among all of the things which are lying around.

Similarly, there are numerous things on the astral plane. The seer will focus on the pentacle—an object, frequently a circular disk with the special symbol of the entity you wish to evoke drawn on it—which will help put the seer's mind in a state receptive to the particular entity you are evoking. To some extent it will also help put the seer into an altered state of consciousness.

5. *Many books describe the use of incense to help the entity appear. How is this possible if the entity stays on the astral plane? How can the entity even smell it?*

The traditional response to this question is that everything has a double on the astral plane. You have probably heard that you have an "astral double." Therefore, the entity you evoke enjoys the astral double of the incense smoke. However, many people no longer believe this.

In fact, the smoke has an effect on the seer. There are three aspects to this. First, the seer should inhale copious amounts of the scented smoke. This will have the effect of *slightly* changing her (most seers are women) body chemistry and thus altering her consciousness. Second, hundreds or even thousands of years of practice have shown that the use of certain scents will help a seer be more attuned to a specific entity. Third, the fact that the seer *knows* all of this will have a psychological effect on her.

WARNING: Many people have suffered dire effects from the "demon CO" (carbon monoxide). Too much incense can result in a lack of oxygen (carbon monoxide poisoning). This can cause brain damage or even death. Make sure that you have plenty of fresh air available whenever you burn incense, especially if you do so in large amounts. Neither the writer, publisher nor distributor of this book will be responsible for any negative results if you do not heed this warning. Take the responsibility for your safety upon yourself.

It should be added here that some ritualists attempt to use clouds of incense smoke in order to give the entity something tangible to use for a body in order to manifest on the physical plane. Although advanced magicians may be able to accomplish this, most who think that is what they are doing merely use it as a background to see onto the astral plane. In short, it ends up functioning in the same way as a magic mirror.

6. *Why do the grimoires give instructions on how to call an entity over and over? If magic really works, shouldn't the entity evoked come to you on your very first call?*

The experiences of tens of thousands of people over the ages, my personal experience and the experience of many of my students, show that magic does work. If you do an evocation *properly*, the entity evoked will come to you. But let me turn this around and ask a question. Why don't you constantly see things on the astral plane? The answer is that for the most part, we are blocked off from that reality because our senses are limited. On the other hand, some researchers claim that our senses are not limited and can normally see and experience far more than we think we do, but our minds function like a filter to block out most of the incoming sensory data (things on the astral plane, telepathy, etc.). Our minds do this, they claim, because our psyches would be overwhelmed if this were not the case. No matter the cause, however, the result is the same: most of us do not have easy access to the astral plane.

The repetition of the evocative calls is not for the entity (who comes right away) but for the seer. It may take many such repetitions along with lots of incense and many moments contemplating the pentacle for a seer to open her psychic vision to that level of the astral plane wherein an entity has come to do the magician's bidding.

7. *"Do the magician's bidding?" Some of the evocations tell you to "command" a spirit. Isn't it wrong to force a spirit to do something against its will?*

Many people use this as an argument against performing evocations. What right do we have to command another being? To explain this, we need to look at the study of the nature of living things.

There is an old story about a scorpion and a frog. They came to a river at the same time and the scorpion begged the frog to carry him across.

"You're crazy," said the wary frog. "You'll sting me and we'll both drown."

"That would be stupid of me," replied the scorpion. "Why would I do something that would result in my own death?"

The frog thought about this and, finding sense in it, agreed to carry the scorpion across the river. With the scorpion on his back, the frog started across. Halfway over, the frog felt a "thwap" and a great pain. The scorpion had stung him.

"Why did you sting me when you said you wouldn't?" asked the frog, about to go under the water to his death.

"Because it was my nature," replied the scorpion, also about to drown, "and I could do nothing else."

Just as we each have certain ways we act and think, so too do the nonphysical entities we might evoke. Unlike humans, however, *they do not have free will.* Like the scorpion in the story, they can *only* do what is in their nature. An entity that can help you with information on how to get money may not be able to tell you how to make friends or find a lover. Each entity has a different nature and personality, but they can only do what is in their nature—they do not have free will to do something else.

In actuality there are currently very few magicians doing evocations. The entities that are evoked are literally waiting to do what is in their natures. Just as it is the scorpion's nature to sting, it is the nature of the entities to want to accomplish what is in their nature. Your calling on them helps them to manifest their natures. Your evocation of them is something they desire.

But nothing of great value comes easily. In order to do evocations you must have knowledge, ability and persistence. You will be tested (they won't come if you do not evoke them correctly, they may give only partial answers to your questions, leading you to error).

Humans have free will and can do other than their natures. You might think of these nonphysical entities as *living computers*. They only work, they only do that which is in their nature, when they are commanded to do so. This is similar to giving commands to a computer. If you command it to print a document and all of your hardware and software is set up to accomplish this, it will print the document. If you command it to fly in the air and change into a butterfly, you will meet failure. The computer cannot do what is not in its nature. Likewise the spirits, the living computers, can only do what is in their nature when you command them to do something.

It is their nature to obey proper commands. The question should not be, "Isn't it wrong to force a spirit to do something against its will?" Rather, we should ask ourselves how we can be so cruel as not to help them manifest what is their nature by evoking them.

TOOLS FOR EVOCATION

Perhaps the most important tool for the magician and seer who wish to perform evocations is the magic mirror. Unlike the usual kind of silver-backed mirror, a magic mirror is black. There are many variations on the design, but here is one that is simple and fairly easy to make. Be sure to read all of the instructions before starting. If you are experienced with this type of construction, feel free to alter the directions as you see fit, but keep the design the same.

1. Cut an equilateral triangle out of a new piece of plywood, although a piece of previously unused,

heavy cardboard could make a temporary triangle. It can be between 18 and 48 inches per side. Sand it and undercoat it with a flat (not glossy) coat of white paint. After it has dried, sand lightly and add another coat of flat, white paint. Repeat until you cannot see the grain of the wood through the paint.

2. After it is thoroughly dry, paint the following Greek names on the board with flat, black paint:

ANAPHAXETON on the left side,
TETRAGRAMMATON on the right side, and
PRIMEUMATON across the bottom.

Alternatively, some hardware or art stores sell vinyl letters that can be applied to your board.

3. Obtain the glass you are going to use for the mirror. It should be circular and fit inside of the letters you have already painted on your board, not covering any of them. About 4 inches in diameter is the smallest advisable size, while 18 to 24 inches in diameter is the largest.

Warning: Be very careful when handling cut glass! The use of gloves is highly advisable. Also be aware that a large piece of thin glass can easily break and the shards will be dangerous.

Place this glass in the center of your triangle. Make light marks around the edge of glass (they should be easy to erase) so you can see where the glass goes. Put the glass aside in a safe place.

4. Using flat red paint, add the name of the archangel MI-CHA-EL around the space where the disk of glass will be. MI should be in the lower left corner, CHA should be at the top and EL should appear at the lower right corner. Again, when the glass is mounted, it should not cover the letters. See the diagram below.

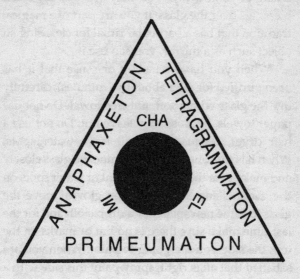

5. Erase the light marks made earlier, then seal and protect the triangle with a flat (sometimes called "satin"), clear finish.

6. The triangle you have constructed is the background for the real magic mirror. To purify the glass, place it under running water and use your mind's eye to visualize any negativity flowing away with the water. You can do this in a sink with smaller pieces of glass. Larger ones will need to be done in a bathtub or shower or even in a stream or river. Do not use the ocean, because the waves will (figuratively) keep returning the negativity you are trying to send away. You may wish to say some blessings over the glass. If you are part of a magical tradition that has a particular ritual for cleansing an object such as a mirror, you can use it.

When you have a feeling or sense that it has been purified (or after about five minutes), carefully dry the glass with a soft, lint-free towel. Do not use paper towels, because they leave lint. Do not use a hair dryer, because that will leave water spots. When it is thoroughly dry, examine the glass closely and make sure that there is no lint or water spots on the glass. Using lint-free cotton gloves, move the glass to some newspaper or a drop cloth and for the last time make sure there is no lint or marks on the top, the side you are going to paint. When you are satisfied that all is right, spray paint this side with a light coat of flat black paint. Do not use a heavy coat, because it might streak or spot. *Hint:* Paint used for making blackboards works very well, although any paint that will adhere to glass will do.

Allow the paint to dry and apply a second coat. Allow this to dry. Check to see that there are no areas missing paint on that one side of the glass. An easy way to do this is by simply holding it up to a light. You may add more coats of paint if you desire, but you must at least have enough so that no light comes through.

7. Get some "mirror mounts." These are L-shaped pieces of metal or plastic that will allow you to attach the glass to the board. Gluing won't work, because you would only be gluing the paint to the board. Use the mirror mounts (you could also use nails with wide heads, but this is not as attractive) to attach the mirror in place (over the area where you have previously erased the marks on the triangle).

The exact number of mirror mounts or nails will depend upon the size and weight of the glass you use. The larger and heavier it is, the more you should use. At a minimum, use two at the bottom and one at the top. Make sure that the magic mirror is secure and will not fall off the triangle when it is being moved.

Important: The side of the glass with the paint *must* be against the wood. In other words, you look *through* the glass at the painted side of the glass. If you have a question, simply look at any nonmagical mirror and you will see that it is clear on the front and silvered on the back. The same is true of the magic mirror, but it is black instead of silver.

This will have the effect of making the black appear quite shiny.

There are only a few other things that you must have in order to perform an evocation. These are:

- The pentacle (more on this later)

- Some candles

- Some incense (frankincense and myrrh work well)

- Some paper and a pen or pencil (in order to write down what the seer tells you are the answers to your questions)

- Eventually you will want to obtain a book with the names, characteristics and pentacles of spirits you will want to evoke. Such a book is *The Goetia* (frequently called, incorrectly, *The Lesser Key of Solomon*) or *The Greater Key of Solomon*.

Also, if you are a follower of any magical tradition, you will use your magical tools. If you are not currently part of a magical tradition, you will not need them. The frequent use of magical tools empowers them and, in fact, can aid in the evocation. With determination and perseverance, however, people without such tools can be just as successful. If you are interested in learning more about the traditional magical tools used by magicians all over the world, you will find a complete explanation in the book *Modern Magick*, including how to make and use them.

BEFORE WE BEGIN, ARE THERE ANY DANGERS?

Unlike invocation, where you invite an entity to take over your body, there is literally no chance of being "possessed" by the entity you evoke. There are, however, some minor problems that can manifest if you do not understand this book completely. By describing them here you will know in advance some of the problems and learn how to avoid them.

1. Although there are many varieties of magic, they all work by directing psychic energy. There are all sorts of minor entities who live off of this type of energy. They are so minor that I refer to them as "little nasties." A friend of mine calls them "astral garbage." When you generate magical energy, they will be drawn to you. They cannot harm you—nor would they want to. Why should they take away a source of the energy they desire?

However, they may amaze, startle or even confuse you. A typical example of such an entity is the appearance—for a brief second and out of the corner of your eye—of someone you know. However, when you look closely you discover that the person is not there. Another example is when you hear someone call your name although nobody is there.

So, if they are harmless, what is the danger? They could pretend to be the entity you are seeking and give you wrong information. They would do this just to keep you working with them so they could continue to absorb or "feed" off the psychic energy created by the ritual. They could put you on the wrong track. If you follow the instructions in this book, however, you will easily be able to avoid any confusion they might try to create.

2. Although *possession* is not possible with evocation, *obsession* is a possibility. In the early 1900s, even some of the supposedly highly-trained members of the famous magical group called the Hermetic Order of the Golden Dawn became obsessed with evoking spirits. This subgroup of the Golden Dawn, known as "The Sphere," became willing to change many of their traditional, tested teachings for no reason other than that an evoked entity known as "the Arab, Ara ben Shemesh," told them to do so. One historian of the occult scene referred to the people in the Golden Dawn who became obsessed with their evocations as "astral junkies."

Can this be avoided? Spiritualist mediums didn't always succeed at this. One of the negative things that people say about mediums is that they would "bring through" the spirit of somebody's late Uncle Charlie, who would then give advice for investing money. This would be in spite of the fact that the man died a pauper. Just because Uncle Charlie died doesn't mean he got any smarter!

So what can you do? There are two things. First, if you ask a question of an entity you evoke, do not assume that the entity is all-knowing. It may be that what you are asking is beyond the knowledge that is in the nature of the spirit you evoke. Second, accept the responsibility for all of your actions. The entity you evoked will continue to exist no matter what happens to you. You are the one who has to live with your decision. Therefore, treat the information from a nonphysical entity as you would treat the information from a doctor, lawyer or friend—consider it, but do not act merely because one person (or entity) tells you to do so. Get a second or third opinion. Remember, even with the advice, you are responsible for your decisions and actions. Do not give that power to another person or nonphysical entity.

The Example of Dee and Kelly

One of the most famous magicians of history was Dr. John Dee. He was the astrologer and advisor to Queen Elizabeth I. It was he who used astrology to determine the time to send out the English fleet against the Spanish. His choice of time helped spell doom for the Spanish Armada. Dee's home in Mortlake, England, held a library that was considered one of the best in all of Europe.

In spite of his great knowledge and talents, he fell victim doing what an entity said without taking the responsibility for his own actions. His seer, the alchemist (and possibly a scam artist) Edward Kelly, claimed that the angel they were communicating with (instead of a magic mirror, they used a large, highly polished black stone—which is now on display in the British Museum—on a table covered with ornate symbols) told them to share everything equally, including their wives. Kelly did not want to do this initially. Dee convinced him, however, that this was something they should do. After all, who were they to disagree with an angel? None of them were ready for this, however, and when they finally did "share everything," it resulted in the destruction of Dee's and Kelly's families and their working relationship.

I urge you to look at the failure of Dee and Kelly and what caused it. Remember, no matter what anybody or any entity says, you are responsible for your decisions and actions.

3. As with invocations, ego-inflation is a possibility. However, the usual type of ego-inflation related to evocation has a different root. When you succeed in communicating with nonphysical enti-

ties, you have succeeded in doing something special, something that few people can do. This can go to the heads of some people. But rather than giving you special powers or abilities, you should consider that this gives you awesome responsibilities to use the information you receive and the services of the entity or entities wisely, and for the benefit of all.

4. Be wary of self-deception. A friend recently told me that she does "invocations and evocations" almost every day. Yet her life is in turmoil and she is awash in uncontrolled emotions. She gives no evidence that she has succeeded in any of these magical activities—in fact, just the opposite.

Several times I have had people say to me, "let's evoke a spirit." But when I ask them for what purpose, they have no answer. If you are going to evoke a spirit, consider why you want to evoke a particular entity and what you hope to learn from it or have it do for you. In this way when you do an evocation you will not deceive yourself into thinking you have been successful when you have not.

5. If somebody performs an experiment in a college science lab and does not get the desired result, people will assume that there was an error by the experimenter. On the other hand, if somebody performs a magical ritual such as an evocation and fails, people may assume that magic and evocations don't work.

This is obviously an awkward, unscientific way of looking at the events. Even so, many people in our society, brainwashed by the unscientific "scientism" that seems to control many people both inside and outside of the scientific community, will try to make you believe this. In fact, if you do not get the desired result after a try or two—a successful evocation—you may find yourself agreeing with them. Such negativity can drive you away from not only magical success, but *any* success. You may feel that if you don't succeed in this you can't succeed at anything.

Such negativity should be fought wherever it occurs! As I've already said, persistence will pay off. If, after several tries, you are still unsuccessful, try changing the experiment. By that, I mean try a different seer. Or if you are a seer, try a different magician. Also try to evoke a different entity.

Be persistent in whatever you do and you will succeed.

Okay, we all know that the above sentence sounds like something you might hear in grade school or at a religious meeting. We have probably all learned that this may not be true in all instances. A person with innate running ability will almost always beat someone with lesser ability no matter how persistent the lesser person may be (although a persistent person of lesser ability may be able to beat a more talented person who is not persistent). As an adult we must determine if our efforts are worth the endeavor.

If you follow the instructions in this book you will sooner or later be able to evoke a spirit. But evocation is only one form of magic. There are numerous others. You do not have to perform evocations to successfully improve the conditions in your life. The book *Modern Magick* describes many such magical systems, including talismanic magic, Wiccan magic, ritual magic, sex magic and more. So let's change that sentence above to read, "Be persistent in your studies and practices of magic and you will find a magical system that can help you improve your life and the lives of those around you."

PERFORMING THE EVOCATION

First, begin by preparing your area. This can be any room where you will be undisturbed for a period. Remember to take the phone off the hook and let anybody else in the area know that you do not wish to be disturbed. The magician will stand or sit in the center of the room, usually facing east, while the seer will be between him and the edge of the area they are using. It would be good to have chairs for both people and a table for the magician. Others may passively watch the ritual. Chairs should be placed for them around the circle you are going to make. You will need to be able to walk outside of any observers.

In the east, outside of the area you are using, place a chair and rest the magic mirror upon it. You may wonder why the mirror should be outside of your working area. The answer is very important.

As already described, some entities such as the "little nasties" will be drawn to your ritual. Therefore, to assure yourself that nothing undesired will enter your area, you will set up a protected area in the form of a circle. The method for doing this is called a *banishing*, which will be described in a moment.

Remember, however, that the mirror acts as a doorway to the astral plane. In evocation you keep everything you evoke outside of your protected area. That is why you keep the mirror outside of the circle.

You should have determined in advance which entity you wish to evoke. A few of these will be listed later, and there are more in books such as the *Goetia* and *Greater Key of Solomon*. The magician will put a pen or pencil, along with paper, on the table in the center of the protected area. (Experienced magicians will use an altar rather than a table.) Two small side tables are also placed to the left and right of the seer. On each is a lit candle. The seer should also have a pentacle or seal for the entity you wish to evoke. She can either hold this in her hand or it can be attached to a necklace.

ATTITUDE IS IMPORTANT

There are two important attitudes that you will need to be successful. The first is that you know that you will succeed. A high jumper who does not think that he or she can exceed a certain height will not make a record jump. If you do not think you will succeed, you will not.

Second, you should understand that this is something very special. You will find that doing evocations will help bring you closer to the Divine. In fact, your protected area, usually called a "magic circle," is as holy and spiritual as any church or temple.

THE BANISHING

The first part of the banishing is to purify yourself. This can be done by taking a shower or bath and visualizing all negativity and cares running down the drain with the water. After the ritual bath, if you have magical clothes such as a robe, you may put them on. If you don't, then wear something special. Remember, you are going into an area that is going to become holy.

There are numerous ways of clearing and protecting your area. The simplest way is to visualize a divine, spiritual, pure white light coming from above, going through you and out to the edge of your area. See it get strong and bright, surrounding both you and the seer (and any observers).

When you sense that this is strong, continue to the next phase.

Those of you who are familiar with other forms of banishings and ritual preparations, of course, may use them. One of the best is called the *Opening by Watchtower*. You will find full instructions for this in the pages of *Modern Magick*.

Another banishing method, one of the most popular, is called the *Lesser Banishing Ritual of the Pentagram*. Here is how it is performed:

1. Start in the center of the circle (the area you wish to protect), facing east. Visualize a brilliant, spiritual light coming from above. It comes into your forehead. Touch your forehead with your right index finger and *vibrate* the Hebrew word **Ah-tah**. By "vibrate" I mean that you should feel it throughout your body and sense that the sound waves goes to the end of the universe. Usually this is done by chanting the word or words loudly.

2. Visualize the light going down through your body and to the center of the Earth. Point down with your right hand, covering your groin, and vibrate the Hebrew word **Mahl-koot**.

3. From your chest, visualize the energy going to your right and to the ends of the universe. With your right forefinger touch your right shoulder and vibrate: **Vih-G'boo-rah**.

4. Similarly, see the energy go to the left, use your right forefinger to touch your left shoulder and vibrate: **Vih-G'doo-lah**.

5. Visualize all of the energy paths you have created, fold your hands at your chest and vibrate: **Lih-oh-lahm, Ah-men**.

6. Go to the east of your circle. (You should be between the seer and the mirror.) Draw a *banishing pentagram* with your right forefinger in the air. Visualize it as a blazing blue energy.

To draw the pentagram—a five pointed star—begin at the lower left, move up to the center, down to the right, up to the side and left, across to the right side and then back to exactly where you began. See the diagram below.

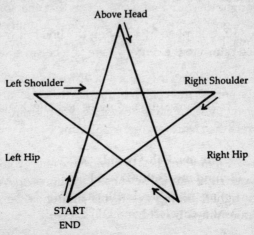

Above Head

Left Shoulder

Right Shoulder

Left Hip

Right Hip

START
END

Now point to the center of the star and visualize brilliant red energy pouring out of your hand through the star and going to the ends of the universe. Vibrate: **Yud-Heh-Vahv-Heh**.

7. Starting at the center of the star, draw (visualize) a bright, white line about chest high. It should be around the edge of your circle as you walk around your area in a clockwise direction. Stop when you come to the south and face in that direction. Repeat step six, but vibrate: **Ah-doh-nye**.

8. Repeat step 7, but move to the west. Vibrate: **Eh-heh-yeh**.

9. Repeat as above, but move to the North. Vibrate: **Ah-glah**.

10. Complete by carrying the line to the east, then return to the center where you began and face east.

11. Visualize huge, glorious archangels at each direction. Say:

Before me, Rah-fay-ehl,
Behind me, Gahb-ray-ehl
On my right hand Mih-chai-ehl
And on my left hand Ohr-ree-ehl.

**For about me flames the pentagram,
And within me shines the six-rayed star.**

Be sure to vibrate the names of the archangels.

12. Finally, repeat steps 1–5.

PREPARING THE SEER

The next step in the process of evocation is to help the seer obtain an altered state of consciousness. During the banishing that has just been performed by the magician, she should have been staring at the pentacle or seal of the spirit you wish to evoke. If you have not already done so, burn some incense. Make sure that large amounts of the scented smoke go to the face of the seer. When you believe that the seer is ready, tell her to put down the pentacle and stare *into* the magic mirror. Then say to the seer in a smooth, comforting voice:

> Stare deeply into the mirror. Do not look at it, but into it. Move the candles on the side tables so that you can see yourself, but so that you do not directly see the reflection of the candles' flames. Stare deep ... deeper ... deeper ...

When you believe that the seer is ready, it is time to move on to the next step.

THE CONJURATION

In this conjuration you are calling the spirit and helping the seer to further attune to the spirit so she can see it through the magic mirror. The name of the spirit you are evoking is left blank. Fill it in from one of the spirits listed later in this book or from one of the grimoires. Words that are all capitalized are names of God. They should be vibrated (as described earlier), as should the name of the spirit you are evoking. Say the conjuration firmly and with authority. While this is a short version (for the complete version, see *Modern Magick)*, it has everything you will need to be successful. With persistence it will work for you.

I do evocate and conjure thee, O spirit _____: and being with power armed from the Supreme Majesty, I do strongly command thee by the most powerful Princes and Ministers and by the Chief Prince I do evoke thee, and by evocating conjure thee.

And by being armed with power from the Supreme Majesty, I do strongly command thee, by Him who spake and it was done, and unto whom all creatures be obedient. Also I, being made after the image of God, endued with power from God and created according unto God's will, do exorcise thee by that most mighty and powerful name of God, EL, strong and wonderful, O thou spirit _____.

And I command thee by all the names of God: AH-DOH-NYE, EL, EHL-OH-HEEM, EHL-OH-HY, EH-HEH-YEH AH-SHAIR EH-HEH-YEH, TZAH-BAH-OHT, Lord God Most High. I do exorcise thee and do powerfully command thee, O thou spirit _____, that thou dost forthwith appear unto me here before this circle in a fair human shape, without any deformity. And by this ineffable name: TETRA-GRAMMATON YUD-HEH-VAHV-HEH, do I command thee, at the which being heard the elements are overthrown, the air is shaken, the sea runneth black, the fire is quenched, the earth trembleth and all the hosts of the celestials, terrestrials and infernals do tremble together and are troubled and confounded.

Wherefore come thou, O spirit _____, forthwith and without delay from any or all parts of the universe wherever thou mayest be and make rational answers unto all things that I shall demand of thee. Come thou peaceably, visibly and affably, now and without delay, manifesting that which I shall desire. For thou art conjured by the name of the living and true God. Fulfill thou my commands and persist thou therein unto the end, and according unto mine interest, visibly and affably, speaking unto me with a voice clear and intelligible without any ambiguity.

Repeat this as often as you wish. Pause after each conjuration and ask the seer if she sees anything in the mirror. If after a short pause the seer has no vision, you should repeat the conjuration. If the seer interrupts you and claims that she sees something in the mirror, finish the conjuration before moving on to *The Questionings*. The grimoires and *Modern Magick* contain more evocations in case you get bored with just the one given above. However, it is very powerful and will work.

If after reciting the conjuration several times the seer has no vision of the spirit (or does not hear or sense the spirit), it is fair to conclude that you are not going to have any success and that the seer is not capable of learning anything at this time. This may be different in the future or if you evoke a different spirit, but at this time give *The License to Depart*.

If the seer informs you that she does see something but it is unclear, you should chant the name of the spirit until the seer says the vision is clear. Once the seer has a clear view of the spirit (or hears it or senses it clearly), proceed to the next step.

THE QUESTIONINGS

As mentioned before, it is possible that you may have made a misconnection and the seer is viewing a spirit different to the one being called. The spirit might also take on a weird or frightening shape. The questionings resolve all these problems.

1. First ask the seer, "What do you see in the mirror?" If the answer is nothing, repeat the conjuration. If she describes a scene, write it down with the paper and writing implement that you brought into the circle for this purpose. If the seer describes an entity, see if it matches the description of the entity given in the book you are using.

If the entity appears in a shape so unusual or weird (as will sometimes happen) that the seer is frightened or upset, say loudly and in a firm voice,

I do evocate, conjure and command thee,
O spirit _____, to show thyself in a fair
and comely shape, without any deformity,
by the name and powers of EH-HEH-YEH
AH-SHAIR EH-HEH-YEH and YUD-
HEH-VAHV-HEH EHL-OH-HEEM!

When recited, the figure should change appearance. If it does not, immediately give the *License to Depart* (given later) and then banish the area. The wrong entity has appeared as a result of your magic.

If the spirit is of a pleasant appearance or assumes such an appearance at your command, move to the next question.

2. Ask the spirit, "What is thy name?" The seer should respond by saying "I feel his name is _____" or "He says his name is _____." In those blank spaces should be the spirit's name.

You will find that the entities do not lie. However, they do not always give a full answer or one that is immediately intelligible to you. As an example of this, a spirit may give another name by which it is known or may simply refuse to answer. If this should happen, say,

> By the power of YUD-HEH-VAHV-HEH I command you to tell us your true name without hesitation or equivocation!

At this time you should get the correct reply. If the spirit gives its name as being the one you are seeking to contact, continue to *The Welcome* below. If not, give the *License to Depart* and banish the area.

THE WELCOME

Welcome, O most noble spirit _____! I say thou art welcome unto me because I have called thee through God who hast created heaven and Earth and all that is in them contained, and because also thou hast obeyed the will of God and mine own will by appearing here now. By that same power by the which I have called thee forth I bind thee for a time that thou

remainest affably and visibly here before
this circle and within this triangle so long
as I shall have occasion for thy presence,
and not to depart without my license until
thou hast duly and faithfully performed
my will without any falsity.

By the power of God I have called
thee! Give unto me a true answer!

Now, state what it is you desire of the entity
you have summoned. Remember, a spirit cannot do
what is not in its nature. Have the seer tell you anything and everything the spirit says, points toward
or does, and write down what the seer says on the
paper you have brought for that purpose. Also
write down anything that you see or experience.

Another thing to consider is that, just as you
are questioning the spirit, it is testing you. The
spirit won't lie, but it may give incomplete
answers. It's up to you to determine if the questions you ask have been completely answered. You
might want to ask the same question in different
ways. After all, acting on an incomplete answer can
cause as many problems as acting on bad advice.

Once you have asked all of the questions you
have and have received the answers, move on to
the next step.

THE PAYMENT

Nothing worthwhile comes without a price. It is
important to give something to the spirit you

evoked in exchange for the information given to you by the spirit or activity it performed for you. This "payment" can be in the form of a song, a dance, a blessing etc. One of the easiest ways to pay for what you have received is to visualize loving energy flowing out of your hands toward the mirror so that the spirit can receive it. When you are finished, move to the next step, which gives the spirit permission to leave.

THE LICENSE TO DEPART

> O thou spirit _____, because thou hast diligently answered unto my demands and hast been very ready and willing to come at my call, I do here license thee to depart unto thy proper place. Go now in peace to thy abodes and habitations, causing neither harm nor danger unto humans or beasts. Depart, then, I say, and be thou very ready to come at my call, when duly conjured by the sacred rites of magic. I charge thee to withdraw peaceably and quietly, and may the peace of God be ever continued between thee and me! So mote it be!

The last sentence in the License to Depart given above is an Old English expression. The word "mote" means "must," so the sentence means "so must it be." The Old English form given above is traditional and adds a certain quality not found in everyday English.

Finally, end the ritual by doing another banishing as at the beginning of the ritual. Make sure that the area is firmly banished and that the seer is out of her altered state. Burn more incense and open the windows. Both of you can have a bite to eat to help ground you and bring you back to regular reality.

THE MAGICAL DIARY

There is still one more thing you need to do. Working magical rituals is identical to being a scientist. You must keep records of all you do. The record of the magician is usually kept in a book called the magical diary.

You should keep more than just your record of the responses of the spirit you evoked in this book. You should also keep such information as the time of day, the weather, your feelings and emotions, whether or not the ritual was successful, etc.

In months and years to come you will be able to refer to this book for information about how you best perform magic. Are you more successful during the day or at night? Does your magic fail during rainstorms or is it enhanced by precipitation? Do you do your best work when you are happy or angry? Over time you will learn a great deal about yourself from your magical diary.

Many people use blank books for this purpose, but the lack of structure can cause problems. Therefore, I created *The Magical Diary*. It has places for all of the appropriate information and instructions on how to keep your record. You simply fill in the spaces. Your local book dealer can get this useful tool for you, or you can order it directly from Llewellyn. See the end of this book for details.

THE SPIRITS

All that really remains, then, is to learn about the spirits and their seals or pentacles. The following is a brief selection of some of the many spirits you can contact through the use of the evocative ritual described in this book.

Below is the seal of the spirit named Bael (pronounced Bah-ehl). It is probably derived from an ancient deity known as Baal, but this is conjecture. Bael is said to have the power to "maketh thee to go Invisible . . . He appeareth in divers shapes, some-

times like a Cat, sometimes like a Toad, and some-times like a Man, and sometimes all these forms at once [!]. He speaketh hoarsely." Further, we are told that the above seal must be worn like a necklace by the seer "or else he [Bael] will not do thee homage."

As said before, the seal or pentacle may be made on paper. In this case a string needs to be attached so that it may go around the seer's neck, but it must be long enough that the seer may pick it up and look at it without removing the string from around her neck.

Obviously, the question you would be asking Bael is, "What are the secrets of invisibility?" You should know, however, that the secret will not make you transparent—it will simply make you unnoticed by those around you. The technique for this may be different from person to person. There is no univer-sal secret for this, so it won't even matter if you share it (unless Bael tells you not to do so), because it may not have the desired effect on another person.

On the next page is the seal of the spirit Amon (Ah-mohn) Amon is great in power and is also said to be very stern. He looks like a wolf with the tail of a serpent and breath of fire. At the command of the magician, Amon will change to look like a man with a raven's head. Sometimes there are "dog's teeth" (i.e. fangs) in the head of this raven.

Amon will give you information on all things past and things yet to be. Thus, if you have a question about the past or about the future you can ask Amon. Concerning the future, it is important to note that we all have free will. We can change the future if we desire to do so. Learning about the future only reveals what is most likely to happen. This information is valuable because with it you can decide to help it along or go against it and change the outcome.

Amon can give information that will help reconcile differences between friends. Amon can also cause feuds. While this may seem negative, sometimes people who are angry at each other but deny that anger can have the rage last for years. A feud or sudden outburst may enable those hidden angers to get out in the open and actually resolve things quicker than had the outburst not taken place.

Even so, the information on how to cause a feud should be used with great care.

The image below is the seal of Buer (Byoo-air). Buer looks like a centaur and should be evoked during the astrological sign of Sagittarius. The symbol for Sagittarius, of course, is a centaur: half man, half horse.

Buer is quite a teacher. He can help with such things as mathematics, logic, ethics, physics, philosophy and science. Buer is also an expert with herbs and can tell you of the secret magical powers that various herbs and plants have. Buer can also reveal the medicinal powers of various plants and herbs.

Buer, it is believed, also possess healing powers, especially over psychological pain.

On the next page is the pentacle of the spirit known as Botis. At first Botis will appear as a snake, specifically a viper. This serpent is quite ugly. When the magician commands Botis to change, however, Botis will take on the shape of a man with "great teeth" (fangs, again) and two horns. Botis will also carry a sword that is very sharp and shines with great brightness.

When evoked, Botis will offer information similar to that of Amon. Perhaps that is why they both change appearance and both have fangs. It may be that a spirit's appearance is related to the information it can provide.

Botis can provide information about the past and future and can reconcile disagreements between friends and foes.

NOW, DO MAGIC!

That's it! With the information in this book you can now try your own evocations. It is safe and the information you may receive is priceless. No matter how many pages I write, however, it is meaningless unless you, the reader, actually get out and do something.

With magic you can improve your life. You can improve the lives of the people around you. With evocation you can learn how to improve your financial situation, bring love into your life and achieve the success you desire.

But none of it begins until you start.

THE ROLE OF AUTHORITY

Most of the people you meet who claim to be magicians are what I would call "armchair magicians." That is, they don't really do any magic. They read about it and talk about it but rarely, if ever, actually perform any magic rituals. Of those people who actually perform magic, fewer still do evocations.

Some do all sorts of rituals, but being ill trained, they only deceive themselves. All they are doing is theater, which may make them feel good but has no objective success.

There are some people who follow the teachings of one particular occult teacher. Rather than really learning those teachings, however (assuming that the teacher knows what he or she is talking about and is not merely trying to make money), they will idealize that teacher. Instead of practicing what the teacher presented, they merely repeat what he or she said. That's not magic—it's hero worship.

Don't take my word or anybody else's word for anything in occultism!

The aforementioned occultist Dion Fortune wrote, "There is no room for authority in occultism." Aleister Crowley wrote, ". . . others have said, 'Believe me!' [Crowley] . . . says '*Don't* believe me!'" I agree with both of these excellent occultists and writers.

Magic, by nature, is *experiential*. It is like driving a car. You can read about driving and discuss it all you want, but you are not a driver until you get behind the wheel, start the engine and drive off. When you drive for the first time you will not be very good at it. You may start and stop suddenly. It will probably take several sessions before you can drive smoothly.

Likewise, you will not be a magician (or seer) by simply reading about magic or talking about it. You must do it. When you practice magic you may discover that you have to do certain things differently for greater success. Real magic is very personal. It is only by practicing magic that you will become a magician. For a real magician, only you and God are authorities, and you are only an authority for yourself.

IS THAT ALL THERE IS?

With the instructions in this book you now have the information necessary to be able to do your own evocations. The technique is safe and has been used by many people in the past as well as by myself and many of my students.

Some people reading this may say, "Well, that's not too much. Is this all there is to magic?"

No, there is much more. Since the beginning of writing, magicians have recorded their theories and techniques. Hundreds of thousands, if not millions, of pages have been written on the subject of magic, both by observers and practitioners of the magical arts. This book is not meant to be a survey or summary of the subject. It is only a small but useful slice of magical wisdom.

If you learned everything in this book, it would be like learning addition, subtraction, multiplication and division. True, you would have the basics of arithmetic, but there is so much more to the field of mathematics. Likewise, once you know how to use the information in this book, you would understand one aspect of the basics of magic, but there is much more to the magical experience.

No single book can ever cover every aspect of magic in depth. This is at least partially due to the fact that every successful magician learns from the past but creates his or her own magical system. It may be close to "traditional systems" (which started as one person's own system) or quite different.

If, as a result of reading this book or out of a previous interest, you want to know more about magic, I suggest that you get a copy of the book *Modern*

Magick. It is large and may look imposing, but it is actually designed as a series of 11 easy-to-understand lessons in both the theory and practice of traditional magic. Once you have mastered those lessons, you will be able to understand and work with almost any magical system on the face of the Earth.

AN INVITATION

One of the goals I have set for myself is to try to explain magic in a way that anybody can understand. It is my hope that if magic is explained in this manner then people will use magic to make positive changes in their lives and the lives of people around them. To do this I need to be in contact with the people who read and practice what I write about. I like to hear from the people who have actually tried the techniques I have described. I want to hear about both their successes and failures. Each can be a learning experience. Even a failure can help a person learn what won't work for that person and can lead to the discovery of minor changes that can result in success. Feel free to write to me about this or about any questions you might have concerning magic:

Donald Michael Kraig
c/o *Llewellyn's New Worlds of Mind and Spirit*
P.O. Box 64383-393
St. Paul, MN 55164-0383

If you wish a reply, be sure to include a self-addressed, stamped envelope for the response, or an international reply coupon if you are writing from outside the United States.

STAY IN TOUCH

On the following pages you will find some of the books now available on related subjects. Your book dealer stocks most of these and will stock new titles in the Llewellyn series as they become available. We urge your patronage.

To obtain our full catalog write for our bimonthly news magazine/catalog, *Llewellyn's New Worlds of Mind and Spirit*. A sample copy is free, and it will continue coming to you at no cost as long as you are an active mail customer. Or you may subscribe for just $10.00 in the U.S.A. and Canada ($20.00 overseas, first class mail). Many bookstores also have *New Worlds* available to their customers. Ask for it.

Llewellyn's New Worlds of Mind and Spirit
P.O. Box 64383-393, St. Paul, MN 55164-0383, U.S.A.

TO ORDER BOOKS AND TAPES

If your book dealer does not have the books described, you may order them directly from the publisher by sending full price in U.S. funds, plus $3.00 for postage and handling for orders *under* $10.00; $4.00 for orders *over* $10.00. There are no postage and handling charges for orders over $50.00. Postage and handling rates are subject to change. We ship UPS whenever possible. Delivery guaranteed. Provide your street address as UPS does not deliver to P.O. Boxes. UPS to Canada requires a $50.00 minimum order. Allow 4-6 weeks for delivery. Orders outside the U.S.A. and Canada: Airmail—add retail price of book; add $5.00 for each non-book item (tapes, etc.); add $1.00 per item for surface mail. Mail orders to:

LLEWELLYN PUBLICATIONS
P.O. Box 64383-393, St. Paul, MN 55164-0383, U.S.A.

Prices subject to change without notice.

MODERN MAGICK
Eleven Lessons in the High Magickal Arts
by Donald Michael Kraig

Modern Magick is the most comprehensive step-by-step introduction to the art of ceremonial magic ever offered. The 11 lessons in this book will guide you from the easiest of rituals and the construction of your magickal tools through the highest forms of magick: designing your own rituals and doing pathworking. Along the way you will learn the secrets of the Kaʋbalah in a clear and easy-to-understand manner. You will discover the true secrets of invocation (channeling) and evocation, and the missing information that will finally make the ancient grimoires, such as the *Key of Solomon*, not only comprehensible, but usable. This book also contains one of the most in-depth chapters on sex magick ever written. *Modern Magick* is designed so anyone can use it, and it is the perfect guidebook for students and classes. It will also help to round out the knowledge of long-time practitioners of the magickal arts.

0-87542-324-8, 592 pgs., 6 x 9, illus., index,
softcover $14.95

THE MAGICAL DIARY
A Personal Ritual Journal
by Donald Michael Kraig

Virtually every teacher of magic, whether it is a book or an individual, will advise you to keep a record of your magical rituals. Unfortunately, most people keep these records in a collection of different sized and different looking books, frequently forgetting to include important data. *The Magical Diary* changes this forever. In this book are pages waiting to be filled in. Each page has headings for all of the important information including date, day, time, astrological information, planetary hour, name of rituals performed, results, comments, and much more. Use some of them or use them all. This book was specially designed to be perfect for all magicians no matter what tradition you are involved in. Everybody who does magic needs *The Magical Diary*.

0-87542-322-1, 240 pgs., 7 x 8$^{1}/_{2}$, otabound $9.95

HOW TO MAKE AND USE
A MAGIC MIRROR
Psychic Windows into New Worlds
by Donald Tyson

Tyson takes you step-by-step through the creation of this powerful mystical tool. You will learn about: tools and supplies needed to create the mirror; construction techniques; how to use the mirror for scrying (divination); how to communicate with spirits; and how to use the mirror for astral travel.

Tyson also presents a history of mirror lore in magic and literature. For anyone wanting their personal magical tool, *How to Make and Use a Magic Mirror* is a must item.

0-87542-831-2, 176 pgs., mass market, illus. $3.95

THE LLEWELLYN PRACTICAL GUIDE TO
ASTRAL PROJECTION
The Out-of-Body Experience
by Denning & Phillips

Is there life after death? Are we forever shackled by time and space? The ability to go forth by means of the Astral Body, or Body of Light, gives the personal assurance of consciousness (and life) beyond the limitations of the physical body. No other answer to these ageless questions is as meaningful as experienced reality.

Guidance is also given to the Astral World itself: what to expect, what can be done—including the ecstatic experience of Astral Sex between two people who project together into this higher world where true union is consummated free of the barriers of physical bodies.

0-87542-181-4, 266 pgs., 5 1/4 x 8, illus.,
softcover $8.95